DISCUSSION PAPER 51

The Social Infrastructures of City Life in Contemporary Africa

AbdouMaliq Simone

NORDISKA AFRIKAINSTITUTET, UPPSALA 2010

Indexing terms

Towns
Urbanization
Urban environment
Physical infrastructure
Governance
Urban development
Social change
Africa

The opinions expressed in this volume are those of the author and do not necessarily reflect the views of Nordiska Afrikainsitutet.

Language checking: Peter Colenbrander
ISSN 1104-8417
ISBN 978-91-7106-678-7
© The author and Nordiska Afrikainstitutet 2010
Print on demand, Lightning Source UK Ltd.

CONTENTS

Foreword 4

Introduction 5

1. COMPOSING SOCIETIES
The oscillating lines of urban consolidation 7
Real power in African cities is the purview of multiple actors 8
African cities remain the preeminent locations for the expression of national aspirations 9
Managing social relations 10
New links with the larger world 11

2. GOVERNMENTALITY
Assessing the performance of municipal governance 13
The prospects for public participation 15
The performative dimensions of governance 17
The infrastructure of cities 19

CONCLUDING NOTE 23

References 24

About the Author 33

FOREWORD

The growth of cities is one of the most significant aspects of the contemporary transformation of African societies. Cities in Africa are the sites of major political, economic and social innovation, and thus play a critical role in national politics, domestic economic growth and social development. They are also key platforms for interaction with the wider world and mediate between global and national contexts. Cities are variously positioned in global flows of resources, goods and ideas, and are shaped by varied historical trajectories and local cultures. The result is a great diversity of urban societies across the continent. Cities in Africa are not only growing rapidly but are also undergoing deep political, economic and social transformation. They are changing in ways that defy usual notions of urbanism. In their dazzling complexity, they challenge most theories of the urban. African cities represent major challenges as well as opportunities. Both need to be understood and addressed if a sustainable urban future is to be achieved on the continent. The Urban Cluster of the Nordic Africa Institute, through its research, seeks to contribute to an understanding of processes of urban change in Africa. This discussion paper by Professor AbdouMaliq Simone, commissioned by the Urban Cluster, is a valuable contribution to shaping the research agenda on urban Africa.

Ilda Lindell
Associate Professor
Leader of the Urban Cluster
The Nordic Africa Institute

INTRODUCTION

Urbanization has much to offer Africa in terms of economic and social well-being. This remains the case despite the clear problems inherent in the ways that urbanization has occurred. These problems include shrinking rural livelihoods, insufficient value-added production, excessive emphasis on rents and administration, and low-cost informal labour. Much is known about all of the things that are wrong, biased, distorted, and underdeveloped in African cities. Yet it is also critical to understand urbanization as a socio-technical process, capable of giving rise to productive relationships among people, materials, and places regardless of Africa's specific histories, political conditions, or position within larger economies.

Lacking in resources, political will, and technical capacity, most African cities — both large and small — have frequently demonstrated a significant ability to link the livelihood agendas and practices of individual households to a broader series of economic, cultural, and religious activities. In this context, individuals take an active part in events and networks and frequent places where many different activities can and do occur. Homes become workshops, workshops become associations, and associations become components of interlinked production systems. Buying, selling, making, cultivating, exchanging, and socializing are tied together in specific, yet changing, patterns of interaction that enable individuals to make effective use of their time, resources, and opportunities (Piermay 2003, Schler 2003). Urbanization, at is its very core, concerns the multiplication of relationships that can exist among people and things and the way in which value can be created by enhancing the circulation of people, ideas, materials, and practices and by using things that exist in more than one way (Amin and Thrift 2002, Gandy 2005, Sassen 2008).

This paper focuses on several key dimensions of urban change in contemporary Africa. First, the city is considered as a locus for the composition of social processes, including the production of specific actors with specific capacities and understandings, and as a site of contestation among diverse aspirations and interests. Second, the city is examined as the site for the application of specific techniques of governance for the constitution and management of populations and as a mechanism that deploys human effort, makes things and built environments, and distributes resources and opportunities. Third, the city is viewed as the locus of physical infrastructure that extends the productivity of existing human endeavour and shapes the possibilities for such endeavour.

The relationship between the character of actual cities and processes of urbanization is never straightforward (Brenner 2009). In Africa, this relationship demonstrates great heterogeneity. There are primary and secondary cities, which are intensely integrated into global systems of transaction — sites of thriving stock markets, built environments, popular cultures. There are others that function simply as large military encampments, where everyday life centres on struggles to seize goods and territory or ward off incursions by others. There are cities with well elaborated policy regimes and others that seem to function through incessantly renegotiated informal accords. Vast disparities exist in the uses of local government budgets. In general, African cities raise 80 per cent of national revues but are accorded only 20 per cent of national budgets. The capacities of municipal budgets across the region also reflect marked disparities. Some cities have invested in cadastral systems that have greatly expanded the municipal budget, while others have initiated land leasing systems and employ other ways to maximize property revenues (Smoke 2008). While these characterizations may serve as a working baseline to anticipate what needs to be done and what outcomes will be likely, stopping the analysis here tends to reinforce the rigid thinking apparent in many of today's urban policy formulations. As coupled human-environment systems, cities demonstrate different capacities to cope with various hazards and stresses.

There is a tendency to approach any analysis of African cities with wariness, as if such cities are always in need of something that is not already present. Cities are machines that thrive through a dense interweaving of bodies and physical and cultural materials and have an impact on regions far beyond municipal borders. Relationships between all things within these borders are shifting all the time: cities can never "stand still." Yet, African cities have long been characterized by a wide range of deficiencies, and these dominate the images of such cities. These shortcomings thus open cities up to various policy interventions, investments, and rectifying discourses that are intended to act as correctives (Bebbington 2004, Hickey and Mohan 2008, Leftwich 2008, Maurice 2006, Mercer et al. 2003).

However, in viewing cities in this way, what is often missed is a sense of their regularity and ordinariness. The fact is they do as much as they can with what they have, with people, institutions, built environments, and social practices, and have acquired extensive experience along the way, eking out a sense of stability in any way they can (Coquery-Vidrovitch 1991). This perspective doesn't imply that the clear difficulties evident in everyday urban life should be ignored. But the difficulties do not "stand alone." Rather, they occasion wide-ranging efforts to protect, compensate for, or change a limited number of assets, to revalue certain aspirations, and to cause events to unfold with particular rhythms (Graham and Thrift 2007; Jacquier 2006).

Well-planned and regulated urban spaces may be less capable of dealing with contingent events, less capable of conceptualizing new relationships with the broader city and world (Legg and McFarlane 2008, Read 2006). Likewise, intensely contested and even debilitated spaces may embody not only resilience, but a determination to incorporate the passions of conflict into more dynamic and stable governance arrangements (Auyero 2007, Hoffman 2006, Schneider and Susser 2003, Vlassenroot and Büsher 2009, Watts 2004).

The key thing is that all cities display particular kinds of vulnerability and strength that require flexible policy and administrative responses. Flexibility is not to be confused with uncertainty or procrastination. Rather, flexibility can be attained through clearly defined, widely accessible options that specify the various trade-offs, advantages, and sacrifices entailed in any consideration of new ways forward. The assumption is that there can never be a completely optimal harmonizing of environmental, social, cultural, economic, and political aspirations — it is never possible to get everything right for everyone. Cities are about conflict, and the point is how conflict can be sustained as a means of putting together the various dimensions of everyday urban life in ways that remake the fault lines and open up new ways of relating for different constituents (Allen et al. 1999, Holston and Appadurai 1996, Iveson 2007).

1. COMPOSING SOCIETIES
The oscillating lines of urban consolidation

The history of urbanization in contemporary Africa has not proceeded in a single direction. Instead, it embodies aspirations and procedures aimed at industrial development, modernization, sectoral specialization, as well as individuated practices of accumulation and subject formation. It also embodies constantly mutating collective strategies for creating spaces of operation and livelihood occasioned by the fluid deal-making that has characterized much of city governance throughout late colonial and postcolonial times (Burton 2002, Coquery-Vidrovitch 1991, Fourchard 2005, Salm and Falola 2005). Cities reflect the countervailing exigencies of economic development, citizen formation, and political control (Bayart 2006, Cooper 2008, Gervais-Lambony 2003). What makes "economic sense" according to prevailing norms, isn't always a good fit with what makes "social" or "political" sense. Cities are thus the bringing together of identities, social positions, and conventions that have been stabilized through different eras and the social ascriptions that have remained fluid throughout them (Hopkins 2009, Myers 2003).

Cities are spaces of exchange, sometime regulated by the price mechanisms of formal markets, but more often through the orchestrating of interactions among discrepant materials, experiences, and positions, whose relationships are not easily translatable into stable forms of comparison and value (Elyachar 2003, Roitman 2004, Verran 2007, White 1992). These interactions produce particular bundles of goods, services, opportunities, favours, and costs that are constantly modified and exchanged. This means that residents not only live in terms of their residential location, work, social ascription, and status, but also are constantly on their way to becoming something other than what they are at the moment. In other words, residents not only attempt to consolidate a specific niche, a particular place in which to live and work, and a stable set of relations. They also seek to circulate across different possibilities, whose shape is not usually clear, but which take at least momentary shape and realization in the process of these exchanges of things and experiences which have no obvious fit (DeBoek and Plissart 2007 , Mbembe 2004; Simone 2004, Telles and Hirata 2007, Walther and Retaille 2008).

Because many cities were built with temporary labour markets, curtailed residential rights, highly uneven relationships with territories external to them, and often fractured linkages with rural areas, they functioned as places of mediation between locality and mobility, always having to find ways of incorporating new kinds of residents and their articulations to other places (Georg 2006, Guèye 2007,Guyer and Belinga 1995, Yntiso 2008). As a result, cities are a context for making claims, for figuring particular narratives of legitimacy that enable individual and collective groups of residents to access resources and opportunities, such as land, services, participation in institutions, and other entitlements (Abbink 20005, Cueppens and Geschiere 2005, Freund 2009, Hilgers 2010, Lund 2006). Particular modes of address are constituted where residents seek to have particular identities and needs recognized. These modes of address frequently change, stretching and shrinking to accommodate or exclude particular actors and territories (Boujou 2000, Hilgers 2008, 2009). As a result, authority is often diffused across sometimes competing, sometimes complementary institutions, replete with different meanings and formulas, as well as different forms of consolidation. Some institutions have formal attributes and structures; others are more ephemeral and dispersed, not easily categorized or defined (Bellagamba and Klute 2008, Kelsall 2008, Lund 2006, Nielsen 2009, Miran 2006, Rakodi 2006).

African cities as places of contestation

There is contestation in terms of the fundamental rights and obligations embedded in relationships between children and parents, between extended family members, between men and women, patrons and clients, citizens and government officials (Marie 2007). Basic questions as to the place of self-initiative, individual decision-making, and the conditions of belonging to family and other social groups are intensely debated. People work out many different kinds of accommodation between the needs of autonomous individual action and the security of life that largely remains rooted in long-term forms of social belonging (Marie 1997, Rodrigues 2007, Tonda 2005, 2008).

These dynamics have a direct impact on what governments and civil society can do in terms of managing and changing urban life. Fundamental issues about what people are able to do together and what they can legitimately do on their own are often replete with tension, controversy, and fluidity. Policy prescriptions that both explicitly and implicitly deal with people's responsibilities to each other, to the state, and to evolving public norms can exert significant influence on how such contestation takes shape and how it plays out. But no single actor or institution can completely anticipate the directions that such a fundamental reworking of everyday life will take. Rather, they risk doing more harm than good in attempting to impose premature solutions or act as if the nature of such important conflict must head in one specific direction or towards a particular resolution (Dorier-Apprill and Domingo 2004, Harrison 2006, Jaglin 2007).

Over the past decades, notions of governance based on the self-initiative and responsibility of individual citizens, the management of delivery systems through entrepreneurial organizations and practices, and the liberalization of regulation as applied to market transactions, have, far from dampening the expectations and demands of lower-income groups, only intensified them. Levels of participation in some form of collective action have increased. While the particular forms of collectivity may not always be recognizable as a coherent social or political force, such collective actions are opportunities for participants to rehearse various practices of negotiation, collaborative exchange, and strategic planning (Brown et al. 2010, Lindell 2010a, 2010b, Grant 2009, Lewinson 2007, Mohan 2008, Ndjio 2005 Yankson 2007). Likewise, just because "governments" are designated as such, with specific legal authority and status as sovereign powers, this does not mean that they have similar ways of operating across different contexts. Nor are those differences simply differences in development stages or sequences that can be captured by auditing and accountability. Governments act differently in different places because they are situated in other relationships. Sometimes ties of common ethnicity will straddle national borders; sometimes governments will attempt to involve themselves across a wide variety of national localities or communities; at other times, governments will pay attention only to specific groups or places. These relationships shape and curtail what governments are able to do, regardless of the prevailing juridical and political frameworks that recognize them as "governments."

Real power in African cities is the purview of multiple actors

While government at both national and municipal levels may have legal authority to operate as the overarching power, in practice this is often not the case. In many countries, the ability of the state to govern still largely depends on how it manages its relationships with external actors, who continue to exert substantial control over the distribution of particular global opportunities for growth (Bayart 1999, Carmody 2009, Pitcher et al. 2009, Prunier 2009, UNODC 2009). States often find it difficult to act for the benefit of their citizens and thus take measures to avoid being accountable to them. Even in cities with highly effective municipal governance systems, the very function of cities as the always dynamic and changing hub for criss-crossing networks and movement flows of all kinds means that much of what is important to city functioning takes place beyond municipal borders.

While governments are equipped with various competencies to shape these external interactions, they cannot completely control the movements of money, people, information, and materials that build, socialize, and change the city (Banégas and Fratani-Marshall 2007, Boone 2003, Engelbert and Tull 2008, Sardan 2009). Municipalities, property developers, foreign and domestic investors, multilateral institutions, transnational corporations, religious organizations, and popular movements may often operate in concert to forge complementary interests, but there is no guarantee that this will take place (Beall et al. 2002, Diouf 2007, Leclerc-Olive 2007, Pieterse 2008, Olowu and Wunsch 2004).

The exigencies of managing scarce resources and fragile political capital has often meant that governments that are supposed to, and indeed intend to, operate with transparency must undertake less than visible actions in order to deal with coalitions of economic actors whose connections, operations, and financial capital remain opaque. Throughout the region, the extraction of some of the most important resources continues to take place through nebulous deals and networks that circumvent existing regulations and accounting procedures (Charton-Bigot and Rodriguez-Torres 2006, Fourchard 2006, Olukujo 2005-06, Sumich 2009). Often, specific national regimes are highly complicit in this process, but for those governments attempting to avoid becoming the simple instruments of big economic players, it is often difficult to fathom what is going on without tying up the bulk of enforcement capacities in a single sector or sub-region of a country (Tull and Mehler 2005, Raeymaekers 2002).

Another important factor is that when city mayors lack widespread popular local support, and where political power is diffused across various parties, factions, or movements, budgetary decisions most frequently are targeted at holding down a workable coalition of political forces. Popular participation in various municipal planning processes often co-exists with parallel systems through which significant resources and entitlements are actually allocated (Dibie 2003, Dubresson 2004, Dung-Gwom and Rikko 2009, Englebert 2002, GTZ 2009, Olukoju 2006, Trefon 2004).

African cities remain the preeminent locations for the expression of national aspirations

Cities enable diverse peoples making up a nation to discover the ability to act in concert and to attain a working sense of responsibility to and identification with each other. In fact, reference to the nation becomes an increasingly practical way in which urban residents, in the face of the dissipation of many forms of mediation hitherto relied upon — family ties, neighbourhood belonging, cultural practice — are able to achieve a concrete sense of mutual connection (Englebert 2002, Fourchard and Goerg 2009, Jewsiewicki 2008, Pype 2009, United Nations Human Settlements Program 2008). That said, urban residents across the region display little faith in the capacity of national governments to realize these aspirations. The implications of this lack of faith are enormous (Bratton 2007, 2008, Bratton et al. 2004, Wantchekon et al. 2007). If a people's commitment to making urban life work is largely based on their belief that the city is the context in which a concrete sense of nationhood can be achieved, and if what can be assumed as the most critical and powerful actor in this process, the state, is seen as an impediment to this project, then what concrete expectations can there be of urban development in the long run?

At the same time, Africa's capacity for debilitating uses of violence — where many actors both in and outside the state revert to violence as a means of claiming rights and resources — is well known. As such, the capacities of large metropolitan areas— full of impoverishment and with uncertain futures — to persist without such violence is a critical basis on which to build new institutions and collaborations. Of course, attention has been drawn to the ways in which cities like Kano, Jos, Freetown, Monrovia, Abidjan, Nairobi, Brazzaville, Goma, and Lomé have been upended by waves of internecine violence. What often passes unnoticed in commentaries about urban life is the enormous work residents do day in and day out to maintain productive relations with each other. While criminality and insecurity may be rife in many cities, and violence easily instrumentalized as a means of accumulation and control, everyday economies require reciprocities, negotiation, and cooperation if they are to be effective.

The ability of cities with millions of inhabitants to maintain these practices over time is a critical resource for any strategy of urban development. The proponents of projects that attempt to include participatory planning, decision-making, and management often express frustration at how limited participation often is. However, this frustration often ignores the labour-intensive process whereby residents are already heavily implicated in each other's lives through the day-to-day work that is necessary to maintain functional relationships with neighbours, co-workers, and extended family members. For many urban districts, what is important is their capacity to keep things moving, to facilitate the flow of individuals and materials in and out, and to maximize the capacity of interchange, even if this is sometimes at the expense of coherence or an ordered environment (Arnaut 2008, Arnaut and Højbert 2008, Nielsen 2007, Mimche and Fomekong 2008, Pitcher 2006).

While achieving appropriate densities of habitation, agglomerated economic activity, and service provision remain priorities, it is important to remember that residents live with often vastly different geographies in their minds. In other words, they live with often highly varied maps about where it is safe to go, which spaces belong to whom, and how spaces are connected to each other. While these different geographies can make planning and administration a challenge, they also can constitute a series of checks and balances that function as insulation against debilitating conflict (Dierwechter 2006, Keith 2005, Marshall-Fratani 2006, Newell 2006, Ndjio 2006). Not content to simply live in well-defined enclaves, residents desire to operate across the city as a whole, and this often promotes a sense of sharing and cultivates places where different actors can witness each other and still have access to areas of safety and more circumscribed practices of commonality.

Managing social relations

Historically in much of rural Africa, the reproduction of social and economic life was thought to rely upon successive layers of indebtedness of individual to family and age grades, family to extended kin, extended kin to various traditional authorities, authorities to ancestors, and so forth. Debt ensured reciprocity and cohesion, but provided little space for individual initiative and accumulation that did not involve continuous giving and taking with others (Guyer 2004, Roitman 2003, 2005).

As a form of social security, such communitarian orientation proved an important structural hedge against vulnerability. At the same time, it acted as a brake on collaborative activities that cut across clear distinctions of obligation and spaces of clan or ethnic affiliation. Cities, then, became places where new forms of both solidarity and individual action emerged — through various associations, unions, demonstrations, social movements, markets, workplaces, and political and religious meetings. These solidarities and activities were put to work so as to use the city as a means of linking various regional economies, actors, and networks (Kohnert 2006, Koonings et al. 2006, Marie 1997). As traditional forms of social solidarity still exerted strong influences, the new forms of urban action necessitated making ties beyond immediate hinterlands. These processes of making connections have now largely been subsumed under the larger restructuring of commodity circuits and resource flows that once again redirect substantial wealth to those that control the machineries of governance (Hahn 2004). They, in turn, selectively remake cities as sites of growing disparities in wealth and ability.

As more money pours into African states to secure access to natural resources over the long term, prospects for enrichment by those in power grow, as do potential threats. As rents are distributed horizontally to allies, these resources resuscitate old forms of the debt system — to regions of origin, clan, lineage, extended family — and reinforce constraints on other forms of social collaboration. As this re-tightening of bounded social worlds is largely antithetical to the efficacy of being in the city, there can be a proliferation of suspicion and distrust that makes initiative and collaboration difficult (Bayart and Warnier 2004, De Boeck 2005, Bosquet 2008, Geschiere 2009, Salawu 2010, Tonda 2007).

Still, as migration and sojourning become more important to residents, and their scope widens, new forms of collaboration emerge to expand the possibilities of trans-local entrepreneurship. Africans are trading goods across different kinds of boundaries and markets, and they are combining skills and experiences from beyond their accustomed contexts, often taking inordinate risks. While these efforts often produce disappointing results, traders continuously try to improve their operations (Meagher 2010). In some cities, major institutions divert their capacities and resources to facilitate trans-local trade, as these circuits come to be experienced as critical elements of municipal space (Simone 2006). The profusion of popular culture and the opening up of everyday life to a wider world of images and meanings — in part generated by the electronic communications between local residents and their compatriots across various diasporas — reorients urban residents away from more parochial ways of thinking about their lives and possibilities (Dolby 2002, Fenn and Perullo 2000, Meyer 2003, Nyambara 2002, Nyamnjoh 2004, Weiss 2002, White 1999).

New links with the larger world

Just as cities continue to be important contexts for concretizing everyday aspirations for national belonging and development, so, too, they intensify their role as platforms for economic and affective articulation with a broader regional and global world. Even when particular cities or districts within cities appear marginal in relationship to the "real happenings" of the world, it is important to understand the ways in which even the most seemingly peripheral areas are linked to substantial powers both near and far.

Certainly, these trajectories of articulation are unevenly realized. The distance widens between the capacities and orientations of the elite and the majority of urban residents. The proliferation of gated residential areas, hotels, shopping malls, and leisure areas not only signal a widening economic divide in cities, but also envision a highly individualized orientation to the city. This orientation emphasizes the elaboration of personal development that is discernable and progressive, but also mutable — able to cultivate skills and persona necessary to move across the city as a whole. This is a city increasingly defined as the seamless interpenetration of work and leisure, optimized performance and self-development, singular style, and proficient adaptation to changing globalized norms. For cities where individuals, households, and associations have been assembled into multifaceted configurations of simultaneous collaboration and contestation — and have generated economies based on and supportive of this coupling — the new developments in the built environment have a major impact on the composition of the city's economic product.

These developments also put added pressure on already highly disorganized land markets. Households become increasingly desperate to secure a parcel in the city, particularly given multiple claims to land and the dearth of clear, enforceable procedures for its disposal. As such, the relationship between household and territory, residence and place, becomes even more tenuous in many cities. No wonder that the attachment to cellular and internet addresses intensifies as a medium of individuation and security. Of course, this massive growth of wireless communications doesn't obviate the "chaotically wired connections" that need to be navigated in order to locate places to live and property to own. While cadastral measures have been put in place in many cities, along with new land regulations and registration procedures, the need for land, and the long histories of its use and division outside univocal notions of property, open the way for constant deal-making of all kinds.

At the same time, these consolidations of new elite territories in the city coincide with the speculative dimensions of urban infrastructure. The rationale for investment in Africa by emerging powers — China, India, Brazil, Taiwan, South Korea, Malaysia, Russia — is not only to acquire assets in extractive and processing economies. Africa also acts as a locus of intersection among complementary interests, financial modalities, and risk assumption. As an exterior in "need of investment," where both risks and potential profitability are high, and where regulatory frameworks are weak, potential synergies among diverse financial streams, competencies, sectors, and networked positions can be explored without long-term commitments or intensive scrutiny. Infrastructure serves as a vehicle of articulation among diverse economic actors. It brings them into a proximity of relations that may be specified by certain contractual responsibilities, investment shares, and tasks, but need not be restricted to them (Large 2008, Mohan and Power 2008, Orr and Kennedy 2008, Sautman and Yann 2007, Stellenbosch University Centre for Chinese Studies 2006.)

If regions, investment streams, regulatory architectures, and production lines are to be articulated in a given place, specific spaces must be configured to facilitate that articulation, as that articulation also exerts a specific range of spatial effects. When different flows of capital, factories, services, communication systems enter a country or urban region, provisions must be made to deploy these inputs in ways that make possible maximum multiplier effects on national and local economies, accommodate the specific conditionalities and aspirations associated with those inputs, and attenuate conditions, barriers, and impediments to their potential productivity. Therefore, to put it simply, they are accorded their space. Theoretically, these spaces attempt to mediate divergent and potentially conflicting trajectories of accumulation and sectoral interests. They also try to integrate investments into an overall economy, while at the same time engineering spaces of relative autonomy — sometimes through a wide range of exceptions and exemptions related to law and regulatory regimes. Practically, then, the implementation of these "projects of articulation" may have nothing to do with the realities of any particular city.

Still, it remains to be seen how this emphasis on producing *grands chantiers* will play out in shaping the social character of the city. Will they introduce new efficiencies — in transport, communication, investment — or impediments? Will they spur new forms of ancillary economic opportunity or further crowd out livelihood practices for the majority?

2. GOVERNMENTALITY
Assessing the performance of municipal governance

Much effort has been expended on getting African municipal governments to be more efficient, law-abiding, participative, accountable, and transparent. The emphasis on "good governance" has become a kind of mantra for dealing with a wide range of problems and potentials. Too often, as a mantra, the invocation of good governance would seem to come with its own clearly defined set of principles and procedures. In trying to incorporate some aspects of Foucault's work on "governmentality" here, it is always important to ask the question, what can be governed, who is to be governed, and how? How are specific individuals, groups, and populations problematized as objects of governmental intervention? How do people turn themselves into citizens or ethical subjects, or refuse to do so? In fact, this kind of questioning is at the heart of governmentality. If we then view the challenges of governance not simply as the application of particular norms and practices, but the formulation of critical questions, then the right to question, the right of residents to raise the prospects of refusing to be governed in particular ways, comes from within the very heart of governmentality. Such questioning about not being governed is not something external to the "game" itself (Cadman 2010).

To approach the issues of governing in this way opens up space for acknowledging the possibility that what looks to be "bad governance" and complicity with bad governance may be something quite different, as residents, citizens, populations try to position themselves within different desires, values, and senses of what is possible or right. This approach opens up the possibility that, despite professed support for democracy as well as transparent and accountable governments, there may be important questions as to how government, no matter how seemingly democratic, may impact their lives. Perhaps more importantly, the notion of questioning as fundamental to governing highlights critical dimensions of the tools of governance.

Significant advances have been made in benchmarking, performance-based incentives, use of diagnostic tools and identification systems, as well as the capacity to link strategy formulation to master planning and capital investment planning. The Global City Indicators Program summarizes a suite of indicators available to the urban sector, from index-driven approaches to standardize and evaluate various forms of development progress, to policy-driven indicators to be used in broad-based consultation and participative planning exercises, as well as performance measure indicators for governance operations. Much progress has been made to end unfunded national mandates, ensure equitable and transparent intra-governmental transfers, and establish frameworks that enable municipalities to access credit markets and development bank funds and to pool municipal development funds.

But these tools cannot adequately grasp how "real" administration of cities actually takes place. In this "real" administration there exists both the intersection and disjunction of different exigencies and aspirations (McCrea et al. 2006, Muneisa and Linhardt 2009). On the one hand, municipal governments are faced with the need to generate income to provide essential services and to pay for the operation of municipal bureaucracies. Staffing levels, budgets, and technical capacities are usually insufficient to do the job of collecting fees, managing traffic, monitoring markets, and regulating trade flows, to cite a few examples. Consequently, management comes to rely on an intermediary sector of brokers and fixers who are not officially part of the municipal system but perform official duties. Because these are not formal sub-contractual arrangements, such intermediaries require certain autonomy of operation as a means of ensuring remuneration for the jobs they do. They have to have flexibility to collect fees, a task that would otherwise not be necessary if citizens dealt with the bureaucracies themselves — if they actually could.

At the same time, the operations of these intermediaries remain subsumed under the overall agenda of the relevant municipal bureaucracy. Autonomy is displayed in the very way these intermediaries demonstrate their access to the bureaucracy — that is, they have access even though there is no formal reason why they should. As a result, the management of various activities — trading, driving, marketing, parking, licensing, or adjudicating — also entails the possibility of "citizens" managing the operations of the bureaucracy through such intermediaries, who are not necessarily beholden to the official rules and procedures. In many ways, then, the governance of the city cannot be subsumed under conventional normative strictures — they simply do not work. At the same time, the techniques of management that interweave official and unofficial practices in order to accomplish the management of particular activities and bodies also give rise to a wide range of seemingly insoluble dilemmas (Blundo 2006, Dill 2006, Laurent et al. 2004, Prag 2010). While clearer delineation of institutional competencies and the availability of more money and technical capacity might bring about more conventional dispositions, these are often blind to dealing with the accumulated histories of this interweaving of official and unofficial practices and the particular subject positions and spaces of operation they institutionalize over time.

On the other hand, residents have to rely on the techniques that available municipal administrations use in order to make lines of authority and responsibility visible, as well as sectors of concern. While aspects of life can seem very well ordered and defined, it is largely only because of the often messy assemblages of official institutions and vast networks of unofficial intermediaries that such an appearance of clarity can be sustained. Residents must thus create and sustain concrete possibilities for mixing up distinctions between residence and commerce, licit and illicit work, religion and secularity, the familiar and entrepreneurial in order to maintain their own semblance of clear identification, agendas, and life strategies. Of course, these actions make it even more difficult for conventional municipal logics to operate. If things need to be messy in order to be made clear, then making things clear may only create more of a mess.

As such, more than simply instituting new administrative procedures, there is a need to completely revisualize exactly what the municipality might look like. Here, for example, the very physical presence of various amalgamations of youth filling public spaces in cities through political demonstration, cultural festivity, and organized intimidation not only becomes a concrete vehicle of such revising, but a reactivation of the nation as platform for reaching a larger world (Arnaut 2008, Hansen 2005, Jua 2003, Moyo 2007). While African governments have often been understandably afraid of the "street" and of youth, this coupling of youth out on the streets is sometimes the only way in which a city is able to see the possibilities of a "new future."

As politicians, bureaucrats, technicians, and ministers in some countries have been known to run the country largely outside the nominal rules and institutions of the state, to what extent do critical interventions in the future of African cities also rely on what can be mobilized outside the state? Of course, this is a precarious issue, as multilateral relationships and development inputs take place largely as a matter of relations between states. Additionally, the widespread proliferation of NGOs dealing with many different issues, ensconced in many different partnership arrangements, and with widely divergent capacities demonstrates the absence of broad-based social and popular movements. No other actors have the legitimacy or the capacity, so far, to act as an overarching instrument of nation-building. The situation is further complicated by the often bifurcated composition of national regimes, where no single body is clearly in charge. Working relationships then have to be forged that are not easily subsumed under clear hierarchies or sectors (Mitlin et al. 2006).

Sometimes, collective bodies play an ambiguous role in terms of national development as they extract certain advantages from the state (Green 2009, Heller 2001, Hyden 2006, Miraftab 2004, Swyngedouw 2004). Such concessions succeed in furthering the bodies' own solidarity but without their assuming much public responsibility for contributing either to the national fiscus or programme development. Take, for example, *L'Union Nationale des Commerçants et des Industries du Sénégal,* which brings together all kinds of small businesspersons, exerts great influence over national economic policy, yet also exists largely to avoid taxation.

Government ministries across the region are now largely staffed by highly trained, competent, and committed personnel — sometimes even more so than in other countries across the world. These cadres are increasingly the visible face of government. Nevertheless, the predominant practices of state politics in numerous African countries — and thus fundamental decisions as to the disposition of power and resources — take place in a political world that runs parallel to the state. While sometimes a world of opaque decision-making, nebulous deals, and arduous balances of competing forces, this parallel domain of decision-making is often more effective in bringing together the different ranges of actors, localities, and tendencies making up the nation than is the official functioning of the state itself. But the problem is that because it is a parallel, informal world, it is not held to account by its citizens.

The prospects for public participation

Because politics are talked about at great length by large numbers of people, it is not so much the case that citizens, particularly urban residents, do not know what is going on. Rather, the point is that this knowledge cannot be used to address the functioning of the formal state. Even if state actors themselves have little confidence in the operations of national government, or, even worse, use the public realm as a staging area for private accumulation, little tolerance can be expected for the organization of broad-based political movements outside the state. Therefore, forms of cross-cutting collaboration and exchange must be built, not only from the bottom up, but in formats and with objectives that do not explicitly seek to build alternative national movements.

Residents of African cities often use very different calculations of what it is possible to do as a means to decide how to deploy limited resources. Residents have to decide whether it is more advantageous to spend sizeable amounts of income to locate themselves in "regular" situations in central parts of the city, or to save income by living in more provisional conditions on the periphery (Englund 2002, Ferguson 1999, Guyer et al. 2002, Owusu 2007, SITRASS 2004.) There are decisions to be made concerning how much to invest in particular kinds of work or business, how much to invest in maintaining kinship and social relations, and whether residents should affiliate themselves with particular forms of patronage. The intersection of the various ways of working out these decisions theoretically provoke a great deal of discussion and, again, questioning. What are the right things to do? What are the right alliances to make? What are the most effective ways to use limited resources to acquire assets? How can these assets be maximized? At the same time, it is these very deliberations that are often shut down by the existing political power. This shutting down of public discussion then disrupts the basic conditions of mediation and problem-solving. The trappings of democratic procedures — through municipal elections and decentralization — often become a substitute for wide-ranging public deliberations on policy (Devas 2004).

Given the critical state of urban infrastructure and economy in Africa, efficiency gains, cost savings, and resource mobilization will only take place by intensifying and extending the participation of residents in concrete activities in which they feel that they are not simply being consulted or manipulated. Residents must be convinced that participation advances the larger project of city-building (Dill 2009, Robinson 2008, Törnquist 2009). The greater visibility of demands for justice, democracy, efficiency, and morality that is taking place across African cities provides a fruitful opportunity for supporting a process in which political contestation can take place in terms of those who have previously been kept out of the process. However, what the poor actually win in such a process largely depends on the existence of political parties and institutionalized policies that backup claims for rights Here, the problem is that more powerful political forces can define the categories and identities through which these claims can be made.

There are no clear-cut ways out of these dilemmas. The effectiveness, for example, of local government can depend on the interactions of a wide variety of factors. Here, the residues of more authoritarian decision-making arrangements may remain important ingredients. Complete dependence on various forms of local democracy can sometimes make decision-making, participation, and service provision more problematic. Sometimes, granting institutional autonomy to health clinics, schools, and other service providers to appoint locally specific staff and devise local operational procedures will effectively harmonize relationships between providers and clients. At other times, such localization may lead to local, largely unaccountable fiefdoms. Here, effectiveness must take into consideration the extensiveness of social movements and political opposition, the personal characteristics of leaders, the scope and content of intersecting networks, and the histories of conflict and complementarity among parallel governance arrangements (Bierschenk 2006, Crook 2003, Gore and Pratten 2003, Klopp 2008, Langer et al. 2007, Piper and von Lieres 2008, West 2008).

It is clear that many urban residents are fed up with how their lives are managed by supposedly public authorities, even when they fully understand and even benefit from patronage. In the face of these dilemmas, individuals flock to churches and mosques as a means of constituting new personal moralities. These are moralities characterized by hard work, honesty, effort, fidelity, and education. These are all components of an emergent, dedicated urban citizenry increasingly capable of securing major development gains. The economies of evangelical Christianity, for example, display the ironies inherent in the usual assumption that domestic savings are weak in Africa: the large sums of money at the disposal of churches reveal the extent to which urban residents are hedging their futures outside their immediate surroundings. At the same time, churches and mosques can manipulate their followers, as well as extract substantial sums of money.

The growth of religious movements, both Christian and Muslim, is having an important impact by reasserting practices of economic advancement outside patronage and communal systems. These institutions also express commitments to the value of hard work, education, and solidarity across ethnic and regional groupings. The degree to which such religious movements can give rise to a new generation of entrepreneurs depends on the extent to which the elite succeeds in capturing these movements for their own economic and political objectives and the extent to which pastors and imams use these movements to become a new elite (Kaba 2000, Marshall 2009, Miran 2003, van Dijk 2002).

Given these realities, it is important to enrol advocates and champions for new ideas and practices of urban development from a wide range of quarters. For public services often are handicapped by problems of moral hazard, delivering the minimum because those they service lack the tools or expectations to evaluate what constitutes adequate performance. Too often, providers and decision-makers have inadequate incentive to align their interests with those of their clients. As such, situations where there are strong moral connections among people, where they have large degrees of autonomy to act upon them, and where not adhering to them has significant implications for maintaining important social relationships may bring about important improvements in social welfare.

That these situations are now often related to contexts outside the local public sphere — in the religious domain and among activist and even traditional associational groupings — should not deter development actors from engaging with them. In this regard, the numerous transnational trading networks that ensure the supply of car parts, electronics, and other household items, as well as manage the movement of large volumes of agricultural products and minerals outside official state channels, and often with state complicity, constitute a largely untapped wealth of expertise and financial capital. How such networks are incorporated into above-board development collaborations remains to be worked out, but the important first conceptual step is to at least include them as possible actors.

The performative dimensions of governance

While governance indicators and normative procedures are important, what is lost is the array of performative tools that governments potentially have at their disposal as part of their capacity to "make things happen." The process by which municipal government accounts for what it does can limit the ways in which government can become a more *visible* actor in the day-to-day lives of urban residents. Government must always consider where it can be *seen* to be actively at work. Of course, municipalities have often been engaged in visible displays that supposedly point to their effectiveness, as well as many kinds of "show projects" and public relations exercises. But here visibility refers to the ways in which various places and people within the city can actually visualize a government at work in the day-to-day operations of the city.

At the outset, this may mean identifying new ways to use existing municipal assets and thus build new categories for urban transactions that work. Municipalities conventionally attempt to recoup lost value due to various inefficiencies by either subcontracting the management of assets to private firms or selling off those assets outright. In other words, municipal assets are recategorized as commodities priced according to prevailing market value, and then supplemented by other considerations as public interest. But this approach is often a limited way to think about resources that municipalities control or have access to.

The question is how existing resources can attain wider and more diverse use and in ways that also diversify potential revenue streams and costs. Such a process would build on the existing ways in which African urban residents use different networks — categorized in different ways, from family members, affiliates, patrons, clients, co-workers, and so forth — to access resources. These resources are, in turn, distributed in quantities that acquire particular value through the flexible use of categories that point to different kinds of social relationships and responsibilities. In this fashion, limited resources can be judiciously distributed by pluralizing the kinds of actors and obligations involved.

Contrary to conventional economic logic, which sees markets as places where those making transactions dissociate the goods to be exchanged from any meaning or network of use other than that of commodity, most African markets have functioned by multiplying the implications of the transaction. The buying and selling of goods are occasions to construct and reaffirm the complicated ways in which people are involved in each other's lives and the different overlapping networks in which people are involved. Individuals enter these "market relations" for many different reasons and to access different opportunities beyond simply a good price or a quick sale, and it is these multiple dimensions that in large part drive the dynamism of such markets (Meagher 2009, Verran 2007).

Municipal institutions always have to figure out what things cost, as well assess the value of the materials they have to work with. Thus, a critical aspect of municipal governance is to flexibly take the infrastructure, services, and other assets it nominally controls and make sure that their different uses come into play and that the different costed values of those different uses can be set in relationship to one another. For example, municipal space — buildings, thoroughfares, schools, clinics, and markets — could be flexibly categorized for multiple uses, each with its own fee structures. The question is how municipalities can use their ownership of assets and spaces to build up more viable urban markets through the use of local practices, social technologies, and information. In part, what is being implied here is a practice whereby municipal governance attempts to find out what it is "really made of." It extends what it can really do by leading the way to recategorize the uses of that which it already controls and is responsible for.

The relative, if not unproblematic, success of Babatunde Fashola in Lagos and Simon Compaore in Ougadougou lies in the way in which a plurality of actual and potential users of municipal assets is taken into account as opening up new platforms of investment. In Lagos, the ability of the state government to extrapolate from how different places and resources of the city are actually used as the basis for projecting requirements for new infrastructure and services has been an important asset in putting together a framework for investment. Importantly, exploring new ways of managing existing infrastructure and building new infrastructure becomes a way by which different institutional actors actively explore new kinds of relationships with each other. Beyond frameworks that specify key principles, such as no tolerance of corruption and transparency in all phases of project development, there are no fixed formulas for the evolution of these relationships.

Lagos State indeed wants to remove infrastructural management from its balance sheets, but is using this objective to experiment with a wide range of possible contractual relationships. Investment options range from equity participation, various leasing options, boards of trade, concessions, and tenancy maintenance.

In Ouagadougou, the tertiary education sector, although not managed by the municipality itself, has been opened up through a series of linkages across municipal agencies and urban commerce in order to make education more relevant to the country's needs. The city government actively provides students and faculty of the city's universities and technical institutions with multiple spaces and with opportunities to practice skills and experiment with innovative technologies. Here, social and economic policy agendas intersect — where local economic development is predicated on expanding opportunities for appropriate training and where training itself is conceived as access to innovative work. While rapid expansion of like initiatives may produce many mistakes and unanticipated outcomes, it is far better to attempt too much than relying on a status quo that is often overly cautious, jealous of its privileges, and threatened by innovation.

While municipal governments have become increasingly subject to performance indicators to measure and benchmark efficiency, working notions of "performance" have also to become more extensive. These entail the ability of municipalities to "perform" in various arenas and to use its "performative advantages" — as a highly visible actor — to forge new relationships across the city that go beyond simple "public-private partnerships" or "intersectoral coalitions." As public institutions adhere to an increasing number of indicators, it is often not clear, for example, whether "outputs" refer to what a particular programme or policy actually does or to the effects of such programmes on the realities experienced by the public, or both. The same goes for "impact assessment," "final results," or "timeliness" (Muneisa and Lindhart 2009).

Part of the rationale of indicators may be to curtail the tendency of public institutions to invent their own legitimacy or efficacy. But, in the very process of trying to make explicit, through a system of indicators, that which these institutions do, a sense of invention is largely maintained. Even when scientific criteria can be stabilized around the statistical robustness of a particular indicator, this does not obviate the need for interpretive flexibility among competing points of view, particularly in terms of what the municipal government actually does and the materials it actually works with. This process of trying to make explicit what is and can be done, then, points to various possibilities where city governments have unanticipated room for manoeuvre. The process of governance contains within it large degrees of uncertainty that can be mobilized in potentially creative ways (Bolay 2006, Duit and Galaz 2008).

The infrastructure of cities

Despite the proficiencies African urban residents have demonstrated over time and in the face of numerous disadvantages, residents are clearly not able to make maximum use of their capacities. Here the story is well-known: high rates of residency in densely populated environments lacking a wide range of facilities; infrastructure and services which require labour-intensive maintenance activities; and too many residents vulnerable to health problems and a concomitant loss of livelihood. Insufficient investment in energy, transportation, telecommunications, and financial regulation and support inflate transaction costs and thus sap the value of local production. Inefficient systems of revenue management short-circuit needed provisioning and investment.

The list goes on to produce a reality in which residents for the most part spend their time compensating for insecure, provisional livelihoods and social conditions rather than building new possibilities for work, education, social welfare, and leisure for the future. On average, less than 0.5 per cent of Africans are added to the water and sanitation systems every year and only 1.5 per cent to power grids and cellular telephone services. Among the poorest 60 per cent of the population, infrastructure coverage is less than 10 per cent. Nevertheless, the steps that the majority of African urban residents take to maximize access to opportunities, income, networks, ideas, capacities, and the world at large constitute an important basis on which more sustained and systematic urban development could take place. The overall cost to Africa of building new infrastructure, refurbishing dilapidated assets, and operating and maintaining all existing and new installations is estimated at almost $93 billion a year for 2006 through 2015 (Foster and Briceño-Garmendia 2010).

Given this situation, the ways in which everyday urban practices question the intelligibility of how wealth is redistributed and security ensured need to be considered. African infrastructural needs are enormous. The shortfall in electrical power generation means that existing economic capacity is underutilized. Intermittent access to essentials makes planning, scheduling, forecasting, and marketing unreliable (Infrastructure Consortium for Africa 2009). Proven skills that could be dedicated to long-range development and growth are tied up in adapting to sporadic conditions and hedging against unforeseen circumstances.

In large part, inadequate access to power is a matter of infrastructural deficit. Yet, significant improvements could be registered by more efficient management of revenues and budgets. Subsidy structures that smooth consumption costs remain largely captured by more wealthy consumers, which in turn forces low-income residents into more informal high-rate vending networks (Water and Sanitation Program 2009). Facilitating broader access to utility networks, where even the anticipated cost increase for household budgets would not exceed current expenditures, could increase overall revenue and permit subsidization of connection costs, which are often prohibitive for low-income households.

Constant mismatches between funding streams and infrastructure development create revenue shortfalls, as high-cost loans and credits are deployed in projects with limited long-term financial yield. Project screening often does not include systematic assessment of anticipated returns, nor does it sequence and synchronize investment streams to maximize synergies and minimize bottlenecks. Existing management practices seem to foreclose a seemingly easy expansion of a revenue base and contribute to overall high energy costs, thus reducing capital investment for improving generation capacity (Nilsson and Nyachanga 2008).

Local dissatisfaction across the region with service levels and costs has increasingly evolved into widespread grassroots discussion about how revenue is used and managed in cities, with increasingly critical points of view regarding the parochialism of decision-making and resource use becoming more prevalent (Gutierrez 2007). While residents have long depended on highly localized authorities and distribution systems to ensure their welfare, they are also increasingly demanding a wider municipal perspective that embodies a more substantial relationship for them to the city as a whole (Owuor and Foeken 2009).

Responsibility for managing infrastructural inputs will, of course, largely fall to national governments, which in the end retain the right to sovereignty and thus the management of the ways and means in which their territories are dedicated to specific functions. Nevertheless, a region-wide urban development perspective might chart potential frameworks of articulation and achieve support for sub-regionally deliberated reticulation systems. It might also give concrete effect to potential conjunctions of nationally planned and implemented infrastructures, filling in the interstices with various feeder systems and connectors.

A large portion of available investments will be directed towards the extraction and transport of natural resources viewed as essential for economies elsewhere. This is an inevitable implication of bilateral accords, which will be pursued regardless of overarching regional interests. Truncated systems and disarticulation will persist as a result. But even if regional coordinating mechanisms of investment must coexist with such bilateral mechanisms, there are still opportunities to "fill in the blanks" — to develop connecting tissues that promote new intraregional densities among previously disconnected territories. Here, cities become mechanisms for anchoring such intersections — giving new importance to a wide range of secondary cities and border towns that straddle the divide between the usual coastal metropolitan regions and inland, often inaccessible, resource-rich areas (ECOWAS 2006).

As urban infrastructure investment in Africa encompasses new circuitries of capital, commodity, and knowledge flows, there are critical questions about the relationship between how infrastructure gets built and how it gets run. As investment instruments diversify — from concessional loans, equity-development funds, joint ventures with private financial institutions, regional networks often coordinated by multilateral banks, and private public partnerships —decisions about risk and profitability have to consider how assets are actually used, what actors assume the risk of ensuring sufficient demand , as well as the kinds of local public institutions and entrepreneurial networks associated with such projects (Orr and Jenkins 2007).

These concerns are particularly critical as the global economic downturn persists. Thus, for example, China (through the China African Development Fund, China Exim), wants to maximize the long-term capacities of infrastructure to expand trade circuits across sectors, manage accumulating African assets, promote domestic capital formation, and coordinate interactions among discrete economic spaces, policy frameworks, and production systems. Instead of simply re-dividing up territories in terms of competing concessions, spheres of influence, and sectors, China, India, and Gulf states are looking at how synergies can be generated from their investment projects — synergies usually associated with notions of the central city.

As various kinds of finance, actors, networks, interests, commodities, and production plants attempt to come together, what kinds of relationships actually emerge? Can these relationships better link a particular city in its entirety to the larger world? Or do they simply compensate for greater precariousness elsewhere in the urban system by jacking up production values in highly circumscribed, well-managed, and guarded sub-territories of the city? Do they put together centres that refer only to themselves and to those centres in other cities, which they increasingly mirror in appearance and function? What are the relationships between various national, municipal, and regional government departments in terms of apportioning fiscal and political responsibilities, and how do these different departments forge relationships with the financiers, managers, consultants, and technical experts involved in linking money to infrastructure to transport to public relations, and so forth? To what extent are the long-term, more informal networks of entrepreneurs and brokers that have been relied on in the past to negotiate barriers posed by inefficient national regulatory frameworks and other externalities marginalized or renewed in this process?

CONCLUDING NOTE

The major metropolitan areas of Africa have largely reached a point where their anchorage of national and sub-regional economies — similar and divergent — establishes a substantial basis to broaden the articulations among them. Their connections to national territories and global economies make them more than nominal centres of administration (OECD 2007). While many national economies may be overly tied to extraction and primary production — short-circuiting the conventional industrial underpinnings of urban growth —sufficient spin-offs have occurred to partly compensate for this.

Urbanization in certain sub-regions certainly is propelling new forms of regionalization and the gradual integration of national populations into regional domains, and is marking out widening corridors that expedite new economic synergies. As such, conceptualizing city futures always has to exceed what takes place within given municipal boundaries. This is particularly the case for African cities, since they will not be major production centres for the conceivable future. Consequently, they must push the ways in which they can be materially and politically implicated in territories far beyond themselves. The basis for this extension will most likely rely on sharpening inter-city complementarities — parlaying differential networks, geographical positions, and historical advantages into new scales of investment in infrastructure, social welfare, and economic capacity (World Bank 2009).

Of course, the fortunes of the region's cities wax and wane according to dynamics far outside their control, as well as to how much residents actually believe in the viability of their futures. Cities facilitate generosity and greed, collaboration and individual parasitism. They are arenas in which individuals can feel they are living in the midst of a larger world, with all the possibilities of consumption available, as if the hard realities experienced by the majority of urban residents simply do not matter, simply are millions of miles away. Of course, to remain within this imaginary of a well-elaborated urban world when one lives in cities sometimes on the verge of collapse necessitates all kinds of shortcuts and corruption. The ways in which these practices have become normalized for so long can lessen the desire of many to do more than toil to meet their everyday needs.

That said, the history of African cities is overwhelmingly about residents striving to "do the right thing." Kids are clothed and fed and made to get to school on time; there are substantial investments in shelter and health; inordinate efforts are made to identify people with talent and skill and make sure they have opportunities to use them. Such pursuits have continued for decades, despite the awareness most residents have that the bulk of these efforts will prove futile. They are futile — not through any fault of the residents — but because political interests have been narrowly drawn, resources have been insufficient, and because the attitudes and policies that informed colonization and racism have not changed all that much.

At the same time, urban residents have demonstrated a remarkable inventiveness in making cities into something that, despite the prevailing conditions and odds, could work for them, could support a wide range of aspirations beyond putting food on the table. Families and households have internalized the obligation to demonstrate their capacity to do the right thing according to the globalized norms of modernity. No matter how much they didn't really believe it, they were always willing to "play at the level of the world, " to how they could be in the world at large. But they would always have to find a way to valorize the "shadows," those practices and approaches that "got them through" in the city, that made the city something vital to them. They know that these shadows will never have the money, status, or support to become a "new norm." Nevertheless, they have to be recognized in some way.

So, often the problems of urban development arise not so much from the lack of capacity as from the persistence of a certain ambivalence about the city remade; an implicit worry that the city remade too much according to modern ways is a city inhabitants will no longer recognize, even if it is in most respects welcomed. Unless the real politics of urban life deals with such ambivalence and accords formal recognition to the ways in which cities have actually been experienced and built, urban development will probably be full of stops and starts and messy twists for a long time to come.

REFERENCES

Abbink, Jon, 2005, 'Being young in Africa: The politics of despair and renewal', in Jon Abbink and Ineke van Kessel (eds), *Vanguard or vandals: Youth, politics and conflict in Africa*. Leiden and Boston: Brill, pp. 1-33.

Allen, John, Doreen Massey and Michael Pryke (eds), 1999, *Unsettling Cities*. London: Routledge and the Open University Press.

Amin, Ash and Nigel Thrift, 2002, *Cities: Re-imagining the urban*. London: Polity.

Arnaut, Karel, 2008, 'Marching the Nation: An essay on the mobility of belonging among militant youngsters in Cote D'Ivoire', *Afrika Focus* 21:81-105.

Arnaut, Karel and Christian Højbjerg, 2008, 'Gouvernance et ethnographie en temps de crise: De l'étude des ordres émergents dans l'Afrique entre guerre et paix', *Politique Africaine* 111:5-21.

Askew, Kelly, 2002, *Performing the Nation: Swahili music and cultural politics in Tanzania*. Chicago and London: University of Chicago Press.

Auyero, Javier, 2007, *Routine Politics and Collective Violence: The Grey Zone of the State*. Cambridge: Cambridge University Press.

Banégas, Richard and Ruth Marshall-Fratani, 2007, 'Côte d'Ivoire: Negotiating Identity and Citizenship through the Barrel of a Gun', in Morten Bøås and Kevin Dunn (eds), *African Guerrillas: Raging against the Machine*. Boulder: Lynne Rienner.

Bayart, Jean-François, 2006, *L'Etat en Afrique. La politique du ventre*. Paris: Fayard, Coll., L'Espace du politique, 2ème édition augmentée.

Bayart, Jean-François, Stephen Ellis and Béatrice Hibou, 1999, *The Criminalisation of the State in Africa*. Oxford: James Currey.

Bayart, Jean-François and Jean-Pierre Warnier, 2004, *Matière á politique: la pouvoir, les corps, et les choses*. Paris: Karthala.

Beall, Jo, Owen Crankshaw and Susan Parnell, 2002, *Uniting a divided city: Governance and social exclusion in Johannesburg*. London: Earthscan.

Bebbington, Anthony, 2004, 'NGOs and uneven development: Geographies of development intervention', *Progress in Human Geography* 28:725-45.

Bellagamba, Alice and Georg Klute, 2008, 'Tracing Emergent Powers in Contemporary Africa: An Introdcution', in Alice Bellagamba and George Klute (eds), *Beside the State: Emergent Power in Contemporary Africa*. Köln: Rüdiger Köppe Verlag.

Bierschenk, Thomas, 2006, 'The Local Appropriation of Democracy: An analysis of municipal elections in Parakou, Republic of Benin, 2002-03', *Journal of Modern Africa Studies* 44:543-71.

Blundo, Giorgio, 2006, 'Dealing with the Local State: The informal privatization of street-level bureaucracies in Senegal', *Development and Change* 37:799-818.

Bolay, Jean-Claude, 2006, 'Slums and urban development: Questions on society and globalization', *The European Journal of Development Research* 18:284-98.

Bojou, J., 2000, 'Clientélism, corruption et gouvernance locale á Mopti', *Autrepart* 14:143-63.

Boone, Catherine, 2003, *Political Topographies of the African State*. New York: Cambridge University Press.

Bousquet, Anne, 2008, 'Développement urbain au Kenya: une sécession territoriale sous couvert de développement durable', *Afrique contemporaine* 226:269-90.

Bratton, Michael, 2007, 'Formal versus Informal Institutions in Africa', *Journal of Democracy* 18:96-110.

Bratton, Michael, 2008, 'Do Free Elections Foster Capable Governments? The Democracy-Governance Connection in Africa', AfroBarometer Working Paper104.

Bratton, Michael, Robert Mattes and E. Gyimah-Boadi, 2004, *Public Opinion, Democracy, and Market Reform in Africa*. Cambridge: Cambridge University Press.

Brenner, Neil, 2009, 'Cities, territorial development and the new urban politics', in Chris Rumford (ed.), *Handbook of European Studies*. London: Sage, pp. 442-63.

Broadman, Harry, 2007, *Africa's silk road: China and India's new economic frontier.* Washington DC: World Bank.
Brown, Alison, Michael Lyons and Ibrahima Dankoco, 2010, 'Street Traders and the Emerging Spaces for Urban Voice and Citizenship in African Cities', *Urban Studies* 47:666-83.
Burton, Andrew (ed.), 2002, *The Urban Experience in Eastern Africa c.1750-2000.* Nairobi: British Institute in Eastern Africa.
Cadman, Louisa, 2010, 'How (not) to be governed: Foucault, critique, and the political', *Environment and Planning D: Society and Space* 28(3):539-56.
Carmody, Pádraig, 2009, 'Cruciform Sovereignty, Matrix Governance and the Scramble for Africa's Oil: Interpretations from Chad and Sudan', *Political Geography* 28:353-61.
Charton-Bigot, Hélène and Deyssi Rodriguez-Torres, 2006, *Nairobi contemporain-Les paradoxes d'une ville fragmentée.* Paris: Karthala.
Coquery-Vidrovitch, Catherine, 1991, 'The process of urbanization in Africa (from the origins to the beginning of independence)', *African Studies Review* 34:1-98.
Cooper, Fred, 2008, 'Possibility and Constraint: African Independence in Historical Perspective', *Journal of African History* 49:167-96.
Crook, Richard, 2003, 'Decentralization and Poverty Reduction in Africa: The politics of local-central relations', *Public Administration and Development* 23:77-88.
Cueppens, Bambi and Peter Geschiere, 2005, 'Autochthony: Local or Global? New Modes in the Struggle over Citizenship in Africa and Europe', *Annual Review of Anthropology* 34:385-407.
De Boeck, Filip, 2005, 'The Apocalyptic Interlude: Revealing Death in Kinshasa', *African Studies Review* 48:11-32.
De Boeck, Filip and Marie-Fraçoise Plissard, 2006, *Kinshasa: Tales of the Invisible City.* Antwerp: Ludon.
De Boeck, Filip, 2007, 'Youth, Death and the Urban Imagination: A Case from Kinshasa', *Mededelingen der zittingen van de Koninklijke Academie voor Overzeese wetenschappen* 52:113-25.
De Sardan, Jean-Pierre Olivier 2009, *Les huit modes de gouvernance locale en Afrique de l'Ouest.* Working Paper No. 4, Power and Politics in Africa, UK Department for International Development and the Overseas Development Institute.
Devas, Nick, 2004, *Urban Governance, Voice and Poverty in the Developing World.* London and Sterling VA: Earthscan.
Dierwechter, Yonn, 2006, 'Geographical Limitations of Neo-liberalism: Urban Planning and the Occluded Territoriality of Informal Survival in African Cape Town', *Space and Polity* 10:243-62.
Dill, Brian, 2009, 'The Paradoxes of Community Participation in Dar es Salaam', *Development and Change* 40:717-43.
Diouf, Mamadou, 2007, 'Social Crisis and Political Restructuring of West African Cities', in Dickson Eyoh and Richard Stren (eds), *Decentralization and the Politics of Urban Development in West Africa.* Washington DC: Woodrow Wilson Center for International Scholars, pp. 95-116.
Dolby, Nadine, 2002, *Constructing Race, Youth Identity and Popular Culture in South Africa.* Albany NY: SUNY Press.
Dorrier-Apprill, Élisabeth and Étinne Domingo, 2004, 'Les nouvelles échelles de l'urbain en Afrique. Métropolisation et nouvelles dynamiques territoriales sur le littoral béninois', *Vingtième Sièclie. Revue d'histoire* 1:41-54.
Dubresson, Alain (ed.), 2004, *Décentralisation et gouvernance urbaine en Afrique subsaharienne: Afrique du Sud (Johannesburg, Le Cap), Ethiopie (Addis Abeba), Nigeria (Lagos, Ibadan), Tanzanie (Dar es-Salaam).* Programme de Recherche Urbain Pour Developpement. Paris: GEMDEV.
van Dijk, Rijk, 2002, 'The soul is the stranger: Ghanaian Pentecostalism and the diasporic contestation of "flow" and "individuality"', *Culture and Religion* 3:49-65.

Duit, Andreas and Victor Galaz, 2008, 'Governance and Complexity: Emerging Issues for Governance Theory', *Governance: An International Journal of Policy, Administration, and Institutions* 21:311-35.
Economic Commission for Africa and the Africa Union, 2008, *Economic Report on Africa* 2008.
ECOWAS-SWAC/OECD, 2006, *Atlas on Regional Integration in West Africa.*
Elyachar, Julia, 2005, *Markets of Dispossession: NGOs, Economic Development and the State in Cairo.* Durham NC: Duke University Press.
Englebert, Pierre, 2002, 'Patterns and Theories of Traditional Resurgence in Tropical Africa', *Mondes et Développement* 30:51-64.
Englebert, Pierre and Denis Tull, 2008, 'Postconflict Reconstruction in Africa: Flawed Ideas about Failed States', *International Security* 32:106-39.
Englund, Harri, 2002, 'The village in the city, the city in the village: Migrants in Lilongwe', *Journal of Southern African Studies* 28:135-52.
Fenn, John and Alex Perullo, 2000, 'Language Choice and Hip Hop in Tanzania and Malawi', *Popular Music and Society* 24:73-94.
Ferguson, James, 1999, *Expectations of Modernity: Myths and Meanings of Urban Life on the Zambian Copperbelt.* Berkeley and Los Angeles: University of California Press.
Foster, Vivien and Cecilia Briceño-Garmendia (eds), 2010, *Africa's Infrastructure: A time for transformation.* Washington DC: International Bank for Reconstruction and Development/World Bank.
Fourchard, Laurent, 2006, 'Résiliences et ruptures en Afrique', *Transcontinentale, sociétés, idéologies, système mondiale* 2:11-20.
Fourchard, Laurent, Odile Georg and Muriel Gomez-Perez (eds), 2009, *Lieux de sociabilité urbaine en Afrique.* Paris: L'Harmattan.
Freund, Bill, 2009, *The Congolese Elite and the Fragmented City: The Struggle for the Emergence of a Dominant Class in Kinshasa.* Crisis States Working Paper No. 2, Crisis States Research Centre, Development Studies Institute, London School of Economics.
Gandy, Matthew, 2005, 'Cyborg urbanization: Complexity and monstrosity in the contemporary city', *International Journal of Urban and Regional Research* 29:26-49.
German Technical Cooperation (ed.), 2009, *Cairo's Informal Areas: Between Urban Challenges and Hidden Potentials.* Eschborn: German Technical Cooperation (GTZ).
Gervais-Lambony, Philippe, 2003, *Territoires citadins: 4 villes africaines.* Paris: Karthala.
Gill, Bates, Chin-Hao Huang and J. Stephen Morrison, 2007, *China's Expanding Role in Africa Implications for the United States*, Washington DC: Center for Strategic and International Studies.
Goerg, Odile, 2006, 'Domination coloniale, construction de "la ville" en Afrique et dénomination', *Afrique and histoire* 5:15-45.
Gore, Charles and David Patten, 2003, 'The Politics of Plunder: The rhetorics of order and disorder in Southern Nigeria', *African Affairs* 102:211-40.
Graham, Stephen and Nigel Thrift, 2007, 'Out of Order: Understanding Repair and Maintenance', *Theory, Culture and Society* 24:1-25.
Grant, Richard, 2009, *Globalizing City: The Urban and Economic Transformation of Accra.* Syracuse NY: Syracuse University Press.
Green, Maia, 2009, *Government through Time: Participation and poverty reduction in Tanzania.* Chronic Poverty Research Centre Working Paper No. 145, University of Manchester.
Guèye, Chiekh, 2007, 'Entre frontières économiques et frontières religieuses: le café Touba recompose le territoire mouride', in Jean-Luc Piermay et Cheikh Sarr (eds), *La ville sénégalaise. Une invention aux frontières du monde.* Paris: Karthala, pp. 137-51.
Gutierrez, Eric, 2007, 'Delivering pro-poor water and sanitation services: The technical and political challenges in Malawi and Zambia', *Geoforum* 38:886-900.
Guyer, Jane, 2004, *Marginal Gains: Monetary transactions in Atlantic Africa.* Chicago: University of Chicago Press.

Guyer, Jane and Eno Belinga, 1995, 'Wealth in people as wealth in knowledge: Accumulation and composition in Equatorial Africa', *Journal of African History* 36:91-126.

Guyer, Jane, LeRay Denzer and Adigun Agbaje (eds), 2002, *Money Struggles and City Life*. Portsmouth: Heinemann.

Hahn, Hans Peter, 2004, 'Global goods and the process of appropriation', in Peter Probst and Gerd Spittler (eds), *Between Resistance and Expansion: Explorations of local vitality in Africa*. Münster: Lit Verlag, pp 211-30.

Hansen, Karen Tranberg, 2005, 'Getting Stuck in the Compound: Some Odds against Social Adulthood in Lusaka, Zambia', *Africa Today* 51:3-18.

Harrison, Philip, 2006, 'On the Edge of Reason: Planning and urban futures in Africa', *Urban Studies* 43:319-35.

Heller, Patrick, 2001, 'Moving the State: The Politics of Democratic Decentralization in Kerala, South Africa, and Porto Allegre', *Politics and Society* 29:131-63.

Hickey, Sam and Giles Mohan, 2008, 'Poverty reduction strategies, participation and the politics of accountability', *Review of International Political Economy* 15:234-58.

Hilgers, Mathieu, 2008, 'Politiques urbaines, contestation et décentralisation. Lotissement et représentations sociales au Burkina Faso', *Autrepart*, 47:209-26.

Hilgers, Mathieu, 2009, *Une ethnographie á l'èchelle de la ville*. Paris: Karthala.

Hoffman, Danny, 2006, 'Disagreement: Dissent Politics and the War in Sierra Leone', *AfricaToday* 52:3-24.

Holston, James and Arjun Appadurai, 1996, 'Cities and Citizens', *Public Culture* 8:187-204.

Hopkins, Anthony, 2009, 'The New Economic History of Africa', *Journal of African History* 50:155-77.

Hyden, Goran, 2006, *African Politics in Comparative Perspective*. Cambridge: Cambridge University Press.

Jenkins, Rhys and Charles Edwards, 2006, 'The economic impacts of China and India on sub-Saharan Africa: Trends and prospects', *Journal of Asian Economics* 17:207-25.

Infrastructure Consortium for Africa, 2009, *Annual Report 2009*. Tunis Belvedere, Tunisia: Infrastructure Consortium for Africa.

Iveson, Kurt, 2007, *Publics and the City*. Oxford and Malden MA: Blackwell.

Jacquier, Claude, 2006, 'Can Distressed Urban Areas Become Growth Poles?' in *Competitive Cities in the Global Economy*. Paris: OECD Territorial Reviews, pp. 381-92.

Jaglin, Sylvy, 2007, 'Décentralisation et gouvernance de la diversité: les services urbains en Afrique Anglophone', in Laurent Fourchard (ed.), *Gouverner les villes d'Afrique: Etat, gouvernement local et acteurs privés*. Paris: Karthala/CEAN, pp. 21-34.

Jewsiewicki, Bogumil and Pim Higginson, 2008, 'Residing in Kinshasa: Between ColonialModernization and Globalization', *Research in African Literatures* 39:105-16.

Jua, Nantang, 2003, 'Differential Responses to Disappearing Transitional Pathways: Redefining possibility among Cameroonian Youths', *African Studies Review* 46:13-36.

Leclerc-Olive, Michèle 2007, 'Urban Issues and Local Powers: Who Can Speak for the Community', in Dickson Eyoh and Richard Stren (eds), *Decentralization and the Politics of Urban Development in West Africa*. Washington DC: Woodrow Wilson Center for International Scholars.

Kaba, Lansiné, 2000, 'Islam in West Africa: Radicalism and the new ethic of disagreement, 1960-1990.', in Nehemia Levtzion and Randall L. Pouwels (eds), *The history of Islam in Africa*. Athens OH: Ohio University Press, pp. 189-208.

Katumanga, Musambayi with Lionel Cliffe, 2005, *Nairobi – a city besieged: The impact of armed violence on poverty and development*. A case study for the Armed Violence and Poverty Initiative, Centre for International Cooperation and Security, University of Bradford.

Keith, Michael, 2005, *After the Cosmopolitan? Multicultural cities and the future of racism*. London and New York: Routledge.

Kelsall, Tim, 2008, *Growing with the Grain in African Development*. Discussion Paper No. 1, Power and Politics in Africa, UK Department for International Development and the Overseas Development Institute.

Klopp, Jacqueline, 2008, 'Remembering the destruction of Muoroto: Slum demolitions, land and democratization in Kenya', *African Studies* 67:295-31.

Kohnert, Dirk, 2006, *Cultures of Innovation of the African Poor: Common Roots, Shared Traits, Joint Prospects? On the Articulation of Multiple Modernities in African Societies and Black Diasporas in Latin America*. Working Paper No. 25, German Institute of Global and Area Studies.

Konings, Piet, Rijk van Dijk and Dick Foeken, 2006, 'The African neighborhood: An Introduction', in Piet Konings and Dick Foeken (eds), *Crisis and Creativity: Exploring the wealth of the African neighborhood*. Leiden: Brill.

Langer, Arnim, Abdul M. Mustapha and Frances Stewart, 2007, 'Horizontal Inequalities in Nigeria, Ghana and Côte D'Ivoire: Issues and Policies', *CRISE Working Paper* 45: Oxford Centre for Research on Inequality, Human Security and Ethnicity, University of Oxford.

Large, Daniel, 2008, 'Beyond "dragon in the bush": The study of China-Africa relations', *African Affairs* 107:45-61.

Laurent, Pierre-Joseph, André Nyamba, Felice Dassetto, Boureima Ouedraogo and Pamphile Sebahara (eds), 2004, *Décentralisation et citoyenneté au Burkina Faso. Le cas de Ziniaré*. Paris-Louvain-la-Neuve: L'Harmattan-Acadámia Bruylant.

Legg, Stephen and Colin McFarlane, 2008, 'Ordinary Urban Spaces: Between postcolonialism and development', *Environment and Planning A* 40:6-14.

Leftwich, Adrian, 2008, 'Governance, the State and the Politics of Development', *Development and Change* 25:363-86.

Lewinson, Anne, 2007, 'Viewing postcolonial Dar es Salaam, Tanzania through civic spaces: A question of class', *African Identities* 5:199-215.

Lindell, Ilda (ed.), 2010, *The Changing Policies of Informality: Collective Organizing, Alliances and Scales of Engagement*. London: Zed; Uppsala: Nordic Africa Institute.

Lindell, Ilda, 2010 'Informality and Collective Organising: Identities, alliances and transnational activism in Africa', *Third World Quarterly* 31:207-22.

Lund, Christian, 2006, 'Twilight Institutions: Public Authority and Local Politics in Africa', *Development and Change* 37:685-705.

Marie, Alain (ed.), 1997, *L'Afrique des Individus: Itineraires Citadins Dans L'Afrique Contemporaine (Abidjan, Bamako, Dakar, Niamey)*. Paris: Karthala.

Marie, Alain, 2007, 'Communauté, individualisme, communautarisme: hypothèses anthropologiques sur quelques paradoxes africains', *Sociologie et societies* 39:173-98.

Marshall-Fratani, Ruth, 2006, 'The War of "who is who": Autochthony, nationalism and citizenship in the Ivorian Crisis', *African Studies Review* 49:9-43.

Marshall, Ruth, 2009, *Political Spiritualities: The Pentecostal Revolution in Nigeria*. Chicago: University of Chicago Press.

Maurice, Amutabi, 2006, *The NGO Factor in Africa: The Case of Arrested Development in Kenya*. New York: Routledge.

Mbembe, Achille, 2004, 'Aesthetics of Superfluidity', *Public Culture* 16:373-405.

Meagher, Kate, 2009, 'Trading on faith: Religious movements and economic governance in Nigeria', *Journal of Modern African Studies* 47:397-423.

Meagher, Kate, 2010, *Identity Economics: Social Networks and the Informal Economy in Nigeria*. London: James Currey.

Mercer, Claire, Giles Mohan and Michael Power, 2003. 'Towards a critical political geography of African development', *Geoforum*, 34:419-36.

Meyer, Birgit, 2003, 'Visions of blood, sex and money: Fantasy spaces in popular Ghanaian cinema', *Visual Anthropology* 16:15-41.

Mimche, Honoré and F. Fomekong, 2008, 'Dynamiques urbaines et enjeux socio-démographiques en Afrique noire: comprendre la présent pour prévoir l'avenir', *Revue Internationale des*

Sciences Humaines et Sociales 02, L'Afrique subsaharienne à l'épreuve des mutations. Paris; Yaoundé: L'Harmattan, 241-64.

Miran, Marie, 2003, 'Vers un nouveau prosélytisme islamique en Côte d'Ivoire: une révolution discrete. In Adriana Piga (ed.), *Islam et villes en Afrique au sud du Sahara: entre soufisme et fondamentalisme*. Paris, Karthala, pp. 271-91.

Miran, Marie, 2006, 'The Political Economy of Civil Islam in Côte D'Ivoire', in H. Weiss and M. Bröening (eds), *Islamic Democracy ? Political Islam in Western Africa*. Berlin: Lit Verlag [for the Friedrich Ebert Foundation).

Mitlin, Diana, Sam Hickey and Anthony Bebbington, 2006, 'Reclaiming Development? NGOs and the challenge of alternatives'. Global Poverty Research Group and the Institute for Development Management, University of Manchester.

Mohan, Giles, 2008, 'Cosmopolitan states of development: Homelands, citizenships, and diasporic Ghanaian politics', *Environment and Planning D: Society and Space* 26:464-79.

Moyo, Otrude, 2007, *Trampled No More: Voices from Bulawayo's Townships about Families, Life, Survival, and Social Change in Zimbabwe*. Latham MD: University Press of America.

Muniesa, Fabian and Dominique Linhardt, 2009, *At stake with implementation: Trials of explicitness in the description of the state*. Centre de Sociologie de L'Innovation Working Paper No. 15, MinesParisTech/CNRS.

Myers, Garth, 2003, *Verandahs of Power: Colonialism and Space in Urban Africa*. Syracuse NY: Syracuse University Press.

Ndjio, Basile, 2005, 'Carrefour de la joie: Popular Deconstruction of the African Postcolonial Public Sphere', *Africa: Journal of the International African Institute* 3:265-94

Ndjio, Basile, 2006, 'Douala: Inventing Life in an African Necropolis', in Martin Murray and Garth Myers (eds), *Cities in Contemporary Africa*. London: Palgrave, 103-24.

Ndjio, Basile, 2008, 'Millenial Democracy and Spectral Reality in Postcolonial Africa', *Africa Journal of International Affairs* 11:115-56.

Newell, Sasha, 2006, 'Estranged Belongings: A moral economy of theft in Abidjan', *Anthropological Theory* 6:179-203.

Nielsen, Morten, 2007, 'Filling in the Blanks: The Potency of Fragmented Imageries of the State', *Review of African Political Economy* 34:695-708.

Nielsen, Morten, 2009, *Regulating reciprocal distances: House construction projects as inverse governmentality in Maputo, Mozambique*. Danish Institute for International Studies Working Paper No. 33, Copenhagen.

Nilsson, David and Ezekiel Nyangeri Nyanchaga, 2008, 'Pipes and politics: A century of change and continuity in Kenyan urban water supply', *Journal of Modern African Studies* 46:133-58.

Nuttall, Sarah, 2004, 'City forms and writing the "now" in South Africa', *Journal of Southern African Studies* 30:731-48.

Nyambara, Pius, 2002, 'Madheruka and Shwange: Ethnic identities and the culture of modernities in Gokwe, Northwestern Zimbabwe 1963-1979', *Journal of African History* 43:287-306.

Nyamnjoh, Francis, 2004, 'Global and local trends in media ownership and control: Implications for cultural creativity in Africa', in Wim van Binsbergen and Rijk van Dijk (eds), *Situating Globality African agency in the appropriation of global culture*. Leiden: Brill, Leiden, pp. 107-46.

Nyamnjoh, Francis, 2005, 'Fishing in Troubled Waters: Disquettes and Thiofs in Dakar', *Africa: Journal of the International African Institute* 75:295-324.

OECD, 2007, *Competitive Regional Clusters: National policy approaches*. Paris: OECD Policy Brief, May.

OECD, 2008, *China's Outward Direct Investment*. OECD Investment Policy Reviews: China. http://www.oecd.org/dataoecd/25/11/41792683.pdf

Olowu, Dele and James S. Wunsch (eds), 2004, *Local Governance in Africa: The Challenges of Democratic Decentralization*. Boulder: Lynne Rienner.

Olsen, Gorm Rye and Ulf Enge (eds), 2005, *Africa and the North: Between Globalization and Marginalization*. Aldershot: Ashgate

Olukujo, Ayodeji, 2005-06, 'Actors and institutions in urban politics in Nigeria: Agege (Lagos) since the 1950s', *Afrika Zamani* 13/14:153-78.

Olukoju Ayodeji, 2006, 'Power Relations in Ward-Level Governance in an Urban Setting: Ajegunle-Lagos (Nigeria) Since the 1950s', in Odile Goerg (ed.), *Pouvoirs Locaux et Gestion Foncière en Afrique de L'Ouest*. Paris: L'Harmattan, pp. 179-208.

Orr, Robert and Jeremy Kennedy, 2008, 'Highlights of Recent Trends in Global Infrastructure: New players and revised rules of the game', *Transnational Corporations* 17:95-130.

Owuour, Samuel, 2007, 'Small and Medium-Size Towns in the Context of Urbanization and Development Process in Kenya', *Les Cahiers d'Afrique de l'Est – Supplementary Issue:* 1-12.

Owuor, Samuel and Dick Foeken, 2009, *Water Reforms and Interventions in Urban Kenya: Institutional set-up, emerging impact and challenges*. African Studies Center Working Paper No. 83, University of Leiden.

Owusu, Francis, 2007, 'Conceptualizing Livelihood Strategies in African Cities: Planning and Development Implications of Multiple Livelihood Strategies', *Journal of Planning Education and Research* 26:450-65.

Piermay, Jean-Luc, 2003, 'L'apprentissage de la ville en Afrique sub-saharienne', *Le Mouvement social* 204:35-46.

Pieterse, Edgar, 2008, *City Futures: Confronting the Crisis of Urban Development*. London: Zed.

Piper, Laurence and Bettina von Lieres, 2008, 'Inviting Failure: Public participation and local governance in South Africa', *Participation and Governance* 1 PRIA:22-42.

Pitcher, Anne, 2006, 'Forgetting from Above and Memory from Below: Strategies of Legitimation and Struggle in Postsocialist Mozambique', *Africa: Journal of the International African Institute* 76:88-112.

Pitcher, Anne, Mary Moran and Michael Johnston, 2009, 'Rethinking Patrimonialism and Neopatrimonialism in Africa', *African Studies Review* 52:25-156.

Potts, Deborah, 2008, 'The urban informal sector in sub-Saharan Africa: From bad to good (and back again)', *Development Southern Africa: Special issue on Living on the Margins* 25:151-67. Accessed March 2010, http://dx.doi.org/10.1080/03768350802090527

Prag, Ebbe, 2010, 'Entrepôt Politics: Political Struggles over the Dantokpa Marketplace in Cotonou, Benin', *Danish Instituter of International Studies Working Paper* 2010:03.

Prunier, Gérard, 2009, *Africa's World War: Congo, the Rwandan Genocide, and the Making of a Continental Catastrophe*. Oxford and New York: Oxford University Press.

Pype, Katrien, 2009, 'We Need to Open Up the Country: Development and the Christian key scenario in the social space of Kinshasa's teleserials', *Journal of African Media Studies* 1:101-16.

Raeymaekers, Timothy, 2002, *Network War. An Introduction to Congo's Privatised War Economy*. Den Haag: Novib.

Rakodi, Carole, 2006, 'Social agency and state authority in land delivery processes in African cities: Compliance, conflict and coordination', *International Development Planning Review* 28:263-85.

Randles Sally, Elvira Uyyara, Evita Paraskevpoulou, Brian Eaton, Ian Miles and Jeremy Howells, 2006, *The Use and Limitations of Indicators in the Context of a City-Region Development Strategy*. Institute of Innovation Research, Manchester Business School, University of Manchester.

Read, Stephen, 2006, 'Towards an Urban Space', in Stephen Read and Camilo Pinilla (eds), *Visualizing the Invisible: Towards an Urban Space*. Amsterdam: Techne Press.

Robinson, Jennifer, 2008, 'Developing Ordinary Cities: City visioning processes in Durban and Johannesburg', *Environment and Planning A* 40:74-87.

Rodrigues, Cristina Udelsmann, 2007, 'From Family Solidarity to Social Classes: Urban Stratification in Angola (Luanda and Ondjiva)', *Journal of Southern African Studies* 33:235-50.

Roitman, Janet, 2003, 'Unsanctioned Wealth; or, The Productivity of Debt in Northern Cameroon', *Public Culture* 15:211-37.

Roitman, Janet, 2004, 'Modes of Governing: The Garrison-Entrepôt', in Steven Collier and Aihwa Ong(eds), *Global Assemblages: Technology, Governmentality, Ethics*. Malden MA: Blackwell.

Roitman, Janet, 2005. *Fiscal Disobedience: An Anthropology of Economic Regulation in Central Africa*. New York: Princeton University Press, 2005.

Salawu, Beshiru, 2010, 'Ethno-Religious Conflicts in Nigeria: Causal Analysis and Proposals for New Management Strategies', *European Journal of Social Sciences* 13:345-53.

Salm, Steven and Toyin Falola (eds), 2005, *African Urban Spaces in Historical Perspective*. Rochester NY: University of Rochester Press.

Sassen, Saskia, 2008, *The Repositioning of Cities and Urban Regions in a Global Economy: Pushing Policy and Governance Options*. Paris: OECD.

Schneider, Jane and Ida Susser (eds), 2003, *Wounded Cities: Destruction and reconstruction in a globalized world*. Oxford and New York: Berg.

Sautman, Barry and Hann Yan, 2007, 'Friends and interests: China's distinctive links with Africa', *African Studies Review* 50:75-114.

Simone, AbdouMaliq, 2004, *For the City Yet to Come: Urban Life in Four African Studies*. Durham NC: Duke University Press.

Simone, AbdouMaliq, 2006 'Pirate Towns: Reworking Social and Symbolic Infrastructures in Douala and Johannesburg', *Urban Studies* 43:357-70.

Smoke, Paul, 2007, 'Fiscal Decentralization and Intergovernmental Relations in Developing Countries: Navigating a Viable Path to Reform', in G. Shabbir Cheema and Dennis Rondinelli (eds), *Decentralized Governance: Emerging Concepts and Practice*. Washington, DC: Brookings.

SITRASS International Solidarity on Transport and Research in Sub-Saharan Africa, 2004, *Poverty and Mobility in Conakry*. Washington DC: World Bank.

Stellenbosch University Centre for Chinese Studies, 2006, *China's Interest and Activityin Africa's Construction and Infrastructure Sectors*. Stellenbosch: Stellenbosch University.

Sumich, Jason, 2009, *Urban Politics, Conspiracy and Reform in Nampula, Mozambique*. Working Paper No. 60, Cities and Fragile States, Crisis States Research Centre, Development Studies Institute, London School of Economics.

Telles, V. da Silva and D.V. Hirata, 2007, 'The City and Urban Practices: In the uncertain frontiers between the illegal, the informal, and the illicit', *Estudos Avançados* 21:173-91.

Tonda, Joseph, 2005, *Le Souverain moderne: le corps du pouvoir en Afrique centrale (Congo, Gabon)*. Paris: Karthala

Tonda, Joseph, 2007, 'Entre communautarisme et individualisme: la "tuée tuée", une figure-miroir de la déparentélisation au Gabon', *Sociologie et sociétés* XXXIX:79-99.

Tonda, Joseph, 2008, 'Les "les anges de la mort" du Souverain moderne. Déparentélisation de l'enfance et violence de l'imaginaire des enfants soldats, enfants sorciers et enfants de la rue en Afrique central', *La Pensée* 354:105-22.

Törnquist, Olle, 2009, 'Introduction: The Problem is Representation! Towards an Analytical Framework', in Olle Törnquist, Neil Webster, and Kristian Stokke (eds), *Rethinking Popular Representation: Governance, Security and Development*. London: Palgrave.

Trefon, Theodore (ed.), 2004, *Reinventing Order in the Congo: How People Respond to State Failure in Kinshasa*. London: Zed.

Tshiyembe, Mwayila, 2006, 'Refondation de l'État africain et mondialisation', *Présence africaine: revue culturelle du monde noir* 173:161-68.

Tull, Denis and Andreas Mehler, 2005, 'The hidden costs of power-sharing: Reproducing insurgent violence in Africa', *African Affairs* 104:375-98.

United Nations Human Settlements Programme, 2008, *State of African Cities Report 2008/9*. Nairobi: United Nations Human Settlements Programme.

United Nations Office on Drugs and Crime, 2009, *Transnational Trafficking and the Rule of Law in West Africa*.

Verran, Helen, 2007, 'The telling challenges of Africa's economy', *African Studies Review* 50:162-83.

Vlassenroot, Koen and Karen Büsher, 2009, 'The City as Frontier: Urban Development and Identity Processes in Goma'. Crisis States Research Centre Working Paper 61.

Walther, Olivier and Denis Retaille, 2008, 'Le modèle sahélien de la circulation, de la mobilité et de l'incertitude spatiale', *Autrepart* 47:109-24.

Wantchekon, Leonard, Paul-Aarons Ngomo, Balaby Sall and Mohamadou Sall, 2007, 'Support for Competitive Politics and Government Performance: Public Perceptions of Democracy in Senegal', Afrobarometer Working Paper 77.

Warnier, Jean-Pierre, 2008, 'Invention des traditions et esprit d'entreprise: une perspective critique', *Afrique contemporaine* 226:243-68.

Watts, Michael, 2004, 'Antinomies of Community', *Transactions of the Institute of British Geographers* 29:195-216.

Weiss, Brad, 2002, 'Thug Realism: Inhabiting fantasy in urban Tanzania', *Cultural Anthropology* 17:93-124.

West, Harry, 2008, 'Govern Yourselves: Democracy and Carnage in Northern Mozambique', in Julia Paley (ed.), *Towards an Anthropology of Knowledge*. Santa Fe: School of Advanced Research.

White, Bob, 1999, 'Modernity's Trickster: "Dipping" and "Throwing" in Congolese Popular Dance Music', *Research in African Literatures* 30:156-75.

White, Harrison, 1992, *Identity and control: A structural theory of social action*. Princeton NJ: Princeton University Press.

World Bank, 2009, *System of Cities: Harnessing urbanization for growth and poverty alleviation. The World Bank Urban and Local Government Strategy 2009*. Washington DC: World Bank.

Yankson, Paul, 2007, 'Street Trading and Environmental Management in Central Accra: Decentralisation and metropolitan governance in Ghana', *Africa: Journal of the Institute of African Studies* 23:37-55.

Yntiso, Gebre, 2008, 'Urban Development and Displacement in Addis Ababa: The Impact of Resettlement Projects on Low-Income Households', *Eastern Africa Social Science Research Review* 24:53-77.

Zafar, Ali, 2007, 'The Growing Relationship Between China and Sub-Saharan Africa: Macro-economic, Trade, Investment and Aid', *World Bank Research Observer* 22:103-30.

ABOUT THE AUTHOR

AbdouMaliq Simone is an urbanist with particular interest in emerging forms of social and economic intersection across diverse trajectories of change for cities in the Global South. Simone is Professor of Sociology at Goldsmiths College, University of London and Visiting Professor of Urban Studies at the African Centre for Cities, University of Cape Town. His latest publications include, *For the City Yet to Come: Urban Change in Four African Cities*, Duke University Press, 2004, and *City Life from Jakarta to Dakar: Movements at the Crossroads*, Routledge, 2009.